Festival Profits – The Guide to Making Money at Street Fairs and Festivals

By Andy LaPointe

Copyright 2014

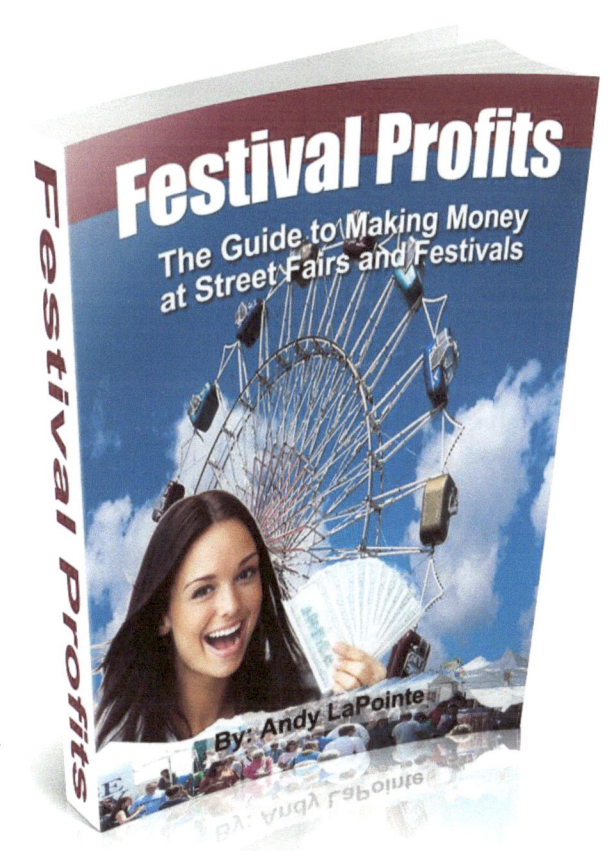

Are you looking to increase your year round income? If so, you can't afford to miss this…

Learn how to market your business the Michigan Way!

Learn a simple and highly-effective ways sell your product year round. You probably already know making money at a festival is hard work. You have load up all of your products in your car, drive half-way across town, unpack and set everything up. All the while, you're hoping is doesn't rain and you have a good turn-out.

Worry no more…discover how to sell your products year round to many of the same people you met at a recent street fair. We call it "Grow your business the Michigan Way". This basically means our great state of Michigan offers unique challenges and opportunities unknown in other states across America. The folks at the website As Seen In Michigan.com can help. They can help you get your products in the hands of year round customers eager to support Michigan-based business. Check them out at www.AsSeenInMichigan.com and www.MarketingTheMichiganWay.com to learn how to grow your business and income the "Michigan Way"

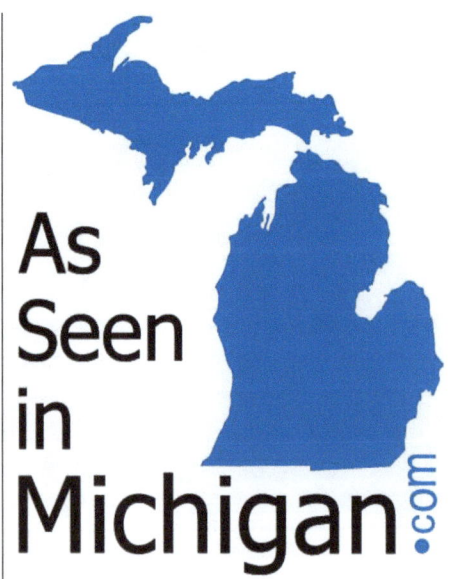

DISCLAIMER:

THE AUTHOR IS NOT RESPONSIBLE FOR THE USE OR MISUSE OF THE INFORMATION CONTAINED WITHIN. THE INFORMATION CONTAINED IN THE BOOK IS FOR INFORMATIONAL AND ENTERTAINMENT PURPOSES ONLY. IT IS NOT INTENDED AS PROFESSIONAL ADVICE OR A RECOMMENDATION TO ACT.

Table of Contents

Bridging the Indoor and Outdoor Gap:

The strategies in this one-of-a-kind guide have been proven successful to work in all festival and tradeshow environments. We have implemented these techniques in both indoor and outdoor venues.

While many of the photos included in this book are of the tent we use for our outdoor tradeshows, they are for example purposes only. The strategies work just a well, if not better during indoor events. The reason is you can get more creative with your merchandising and layout since you don't have to worry about the weather conditions when setting up and staffing your booth.

If you are attending an indoor show, as you read through this information, write down how you would implement the strategies to fit the indoor event, too.

Background:

This is the vendor edition of the Festival Profits System and was written by Andy LaPointe. You can learn more about the entire Festival Profits system at www.FestivalProfits.com

Mr. LaPointe lives in Northern Michigan near the city of Traverse City. The author owns a company called Traverse Bay Farms / Fruit Advantage. This company offers a complete line of gourmet fruit and super fruit products and is distributed throughout the U.S. and several countries across the globe.

In addition to owning and operating a physical store, the author attends numerous fairs and festivals across Michigan and beyond as a vendor. The information is this special report is time tested and proven with real world experience both with working as a business owner and attending events as a vendor.

In addition to offering training to festival vendors, Mr. LaPointe provides social media consulting and Internet consulting to street fair vendors and small business owners.

Introduction

Participating in local fairs and festivals is an excellent way to support your local community and grow your business. However, unless you have a proven road map to follow, you may not being taking full advantage of the money making and list building opportunity of being a vendor at a festival.

In the following pages of this module, you'll discover some of the best tips and strategies to integrate your offline business with time tested online marketing techniques to take full advantage of the customers you meet at a festival. This information will not only provide you the tools you need to explode your sales during the event but all year long. This special module will provide you with proven, step-by-step strategies you can implement immediately and at virtually zero cost.

Here is an overview of some of the concepts you will learn:

How to:

1. Maximum your sales and profits in the 100 square feet you own during the fair
2. Create an email list - Capture contact information easily
3. Offer high value, free gifts to encourage repeat business
4. Spread the word about your business and make it go viral
5. Use leverage to grow your list
6. Measure and improve profitability

So let's get started…

Your World is only 10' x 10'

As a festival vendor your world is only 10' x 10' (sometimes 12' x 12') but no usually more. Unless you pay for two spaces or slots, you only have 100 square feet to persuade people to stop at your booth and spend their money with you and not with other vendors.

One of the best things to remember is even if you are the only vendor selling your type of product (jewelry, shirts, engraved mirrors, marsh mellow guns, etc.) you still have competition. You may not have direct competition (other vendors selling exactly what you are selling) but in reality every other vendor at the event is your competition.

Remember, every person that attends a festival only has a limited amount of money to spend. Even if they absolutely "love" your product, if they already spent their money with another vendor they can't buy from you no matter how much they want to. That is why the techniques in the module are vital to your success. You'll learn how to make your products so irresistible the people must have it. They'll gladly spend some of their limited about of money at your booth and be happy they did.

One of the most important secrets you need to understand as a festival vendor is people walk "tent row" in an attempt to discover a hidden gem. They truly enjoy spending a Saturday afternoon wandering through though "tent city" to purchase products they may have never known existed. When they do see something unique they will buy it. So the first step to making money is to get people to stop at your booth.

How to Get People to Bee-Line to Your Tent?

Here are some ideas to grab to attentions of festival visitors so they will make a bee-line to your booth. First and foremost, your booth must address two critical issues:

1. The exterior of your booth must be eye catching. It must catch the eye of attendee that are at least 50 feet away.
2. The interior of your tent must maintain their interest so you can engage them with meaningful discussion. I'll go into further detail later about what I mean by "meaningful discussion". But no matter what you are selling the interior of your booth must be interesting.

Here are some of the areas to consider for the exterior of your booth:

- Your canopy
- A Booth Sign
- A Street Sign
- Your side and back walls

Here are some of the areas to consider for the interior of your booth:

- Your booth layout
- Product photos
- If applicable, mirror
- If applicable, digital camera
- If applicable, product sampling

The Exterior - Your Canopy

Let's take a closer look at the exterior of your booth. The first area to consider is your canopy or your tent. Vendor canopies are available in a number of different colors including white, gold, blue, red and even branded with the logo of your favorite college or professional sports team.

However, unless you are selling memorabilia of a specific college or professional sports team I would recommend not purchasing a tent with a specific team logo on your canopy. The reason is simple. Although, you may be showing your team spirit by displaying your favorite team colors, I guarantee you will lose business. Simply put, some people will refuse to purchase from a business that supports rival team. Remember what the primary reason you are attending the festival. The reason you are attending the festival is to make money. Once you have made the money, you can always go and buy a team shirt and proudly wear it while you are not at the festival.

We use a standard 10' x 10' tent and a few tables for all of our events. That is all we need. We don't need any extra special features like electricity, wood shelving or peg boards. Our booth has a very "homey" feel to it and that works for us. In addition to the basics, we take usually take two full pallets of salsa with us to each festival each pallet has 40 – 50 cases of salsa each case weighing 20 lbs. However, if your booth does require wooden displays, wire racks, etc. you still need to pay extra making your tent stand out.

So what is the best way to stand out in "tent city"?

The best way to stand out from the crowd is to purchase a colored canopy. The color of our primary canopy is red. A red canopy really sticks out in the crowd when over 90% of all of the other canopies are white. Here is a photo of a recent street fair we attended. As you can see from the photo below, our red canopy really stands out from all of the other tents. Is having a colored canopy enough to make more people stop by your tent? The answer is probably not, but it is enough to make your tent attract a little more attention? Yes. So if having a color canopy attracts just one more person to stop and buy, that means you have made 8 more additional sales during an eight hour event.

Remember, it is the small things that can make a huge difference.

Booth Sign

A booth sign is a sign you attach to the exterior of your tent. The purpose of a booth sign is to tell fair goers what you are selling. The next time you attend a fair take a few extra minutes to notice how many of the other vendors actually have any sort of sign on the exterior of their tents. Other than the lemonade and popcorn vendors, I have noticed that only 10% - 15% off all of the vendors have signs telling what they have to offer. To prove my point, take another look at the photo above and see how many have a booth sign.

For example, we have a sign on our tent that says "Salsa Bar". Our customers have told us they noticed our signs up to 20 yards away and the only reason they visited our booth was because of the sign. Here is a photo of our booth sign. As you can see from the photo below it is very noticeable. In addition, people know exactly what we are offering. (The sign in this photo is a cloth sign with embroidered letters. This is attached to our tent with oversize safety pins)

Here are some ideas you can use for your booth sign:

- Jewelry and Necklaces
- Custom T-Shirts
- Marsh Mellow Guns
- Custom Face Painting

As you can see, it does have the be fancy, but it has to tell attendees what you are selling.

Here are some examples of what not to have on your sign. These are examples of what vendors have printed on signs on the exterior of tents at some shows I recently attended:

- Fun and Sassy
- Only Purple Stuff
- Everything 50% Off

As you can see, these types of sign don't describe what is being offered. If people don't what know you have, they won't go out their way to visit your booth.

However, creating a sign can be expensive and attaching to your tent can be difficult, so here is a low cost way to create an attach a sign to your booth for your very next show:

1. Visit a local office supply store and have them create, print and laminate simple 6" x 17" sign.
2. Buy some heavy duty magnets from the same store. These usually come in packets of 8 or 12 magnets per package.

3. Place one magnet in each of the four corners. One on the outside of the sign and one on the inside of your tent. The strength of the magnets will keep your sign attached to the tent and is easy to remove.

Here is what out magnet attached sign looks like:

You can see the magnets on each of the corners. (The upper left magnet slid down a little just prior to when this picture was taken, but you get the idea)

Street Sign

Here is another really cool trick that gets a lot of attention. A street sign will draw additional attention to your tent. A street sign is a 12' – 14' sign post that is attached to the corner of the front post of your tent. The pole can be made out of PVC pipe or wood. Here is an example of our street sign. The sign is a blurry in this photo but you still get the idea of having the street sign for your tent.

You may need to check with the event organizers to see if they allow street signs. In addition, for your safety you should completely remove your street sign in the event of stormy weathering, especially thunder and lightning storms.

The Exterior - Your Side and Back Walls.

Unless you have specific reasons (theft, weather, wind, breakage, etc) for keeping your side and back walls down during festival hours, I recommend you keep your side and back walls tied up. An open tent provides an open and welcoming environment for your shoppers.

The Interior of your Booth

The interior of your booth is in-essence your retail store. However, many vendors miss the point that it is the interior of your booth that truly makes that sale. It is where customers get to experience your business. If your booth has half-eaten sandwiches or trash on your table, is unorganized or messy, potential customers will simply disappear back into the ever flowing crowd in front of your booth.

Here are some points to consider for the interior of your booth:

- Your creation story
- Your booth layout
- Product posters and banners
- If applicable, mirror
- If applicable, product sampling
- A trash can under your table

Your Creation Story

As people enter your booth you need to engage them in a unique and creative way. One of the best ways of doing this is with a unique creation story. A creation story is the story behind your product. In other words, what makes your product unique? So unique that people must buy it that day. This is way your creation story is vital.

Remember what really makes people buy is not your product, but the story of your product. Your product must have story behind it. People love stories. They want to know how you started making your craft. They want to know why you are spending your Saturday afternoon sitting behind a table selling products. Please don't tell them it's because you need the money. Potential customers want to hear your story because they want to be able to brag about the unique gem they discovered to their co-workers when they go back to work on Monday morning. Tell them how:

- Your jelly recipe a secret recipe passed down from your great-grandmother.
- You learned to sew hand-crafted quilts from a wise-old Native American Indian woman during a vacation to the Black Hills.
- You only use the wool from local sheep in your hand knit sweaters.

Your creation story will not only encourage people to buy the day of the event, but to possibly buy more from you.

A creation story has two components:

1. Attention grabbing opener
2. The creation story itself

Attention Grabbing Opener

The purpose of the opener is to immediately engage a customer that enters your booth or stops in front of your tent to view your products. The opening statement can be in the form of a question or a statement. Your opening statement or question must immediately give potential customers insight into what you are offering. Your opening statement must wrap your entire creation story into a single sentence.

Here are few examples of attention grabbing statements:

- Hand-crafted rugs: These designs are inspired by a Native American tribe in the Black Hills. Would you like to hear what each design represents to this Native American tribe?
- Jam and Jellies: Would you be interested in sampling a secret family recipe for apple butter? My
- Hand-crafted stained glass: It takes over 25 hours of intense work to make a single piece of stained glass. Would you like to see my latest work?
- Personalized signs: These signs look great both inside and outside the home. Would a sign like this go in a special room in your house or in the basement?

After reading the above statements, you can see the only purpose of the opening statement is to start a conversation with potential customers. Once you have engaged a potential customer with your opening statement you can tell them about your creation story. Here is an example for your review:

You - Would you be interested in sampling a secret family recipe for apple butter?

Customer – Hmmm, I guess I would like a sample.

You – (as they are enjoying the free sample) This recipe has been passed down from my great grandmother. What makes this recipe so special is how it captures the true essence of the apple. It tastes like the apples were picked yesterday. It always seems that recipes passed down from grandmothers always taste better than the recipes of today, don't they?

Customer – An inaudible sign of agreement as they are eating your free samples and they are still standing at your booth.

You – I remember when my grandmother first taught me this recipe. I remember her peeling the apples in the kitchen with a hand peeler. In fact, here is that hand peeler (have a picture of the peeler on your table – *creates an emotional bond*) It seems the magic of that hand peeler is still in every batch I make today… (Continue with your creation story)

Since many vendors don't have a well thought out creation story, here is the alternative approach way many vendor engage a potential customer when they stop by their booth:

You – How are you doing?; or Nice day isn't it?:

Customer – The potential customer doesn't make eye contact, doesn't reply to the uninteresting comment, turns and walks away never to return.

Now that you have an attention grabbing opener, let's focus on the creation story.

The Creation Story

A good creation story should be information packed and concise. Your creation story should only have three bullet points and take you less than a minute to deliver. The reason is simple. People at festivals don't want to spend the time at any one booth when they have over 100 other booths to discover. Your story needs to be engaging.

Here are the three bullet points for an apple butter product.

- The first time my grandmother made this recipe was over 50 years ago
- My grandmother taught me only to use fresh apples from local orchards. She said local is always better.
- We only make our apple butter in small batches to ensure quality and great taste. In fact, I still have a photo of my grandmother in my kitchen to ensure I stay true to her recipe.

As mentioned above, the alternative to not having an opening statement and a creation story is to engage in polite small talk about the weather. At times, small talk is appropriate, but remember people are attending the festival to discover a gem and spend money, not talk about the weather. Your job is to help them to truly understand the unique features and benefits of your products. They will be glad you did.

Here are some questions you can use to get started in creating the story of your products:

1. How did you get started creating your product?
2. What is the source of your material? (local or imported)
3. What is your inspiration?

Up to this point, you have learned some strategies and techniques to attract people into your booth, so let's turn our attention to the interior of your booth.

Your Booth Layout

The type of product you are selling really determines the layout of your booth. If you have a product to sample, i.e. fudge, salsas, jellies, etc. you may want to consider the sampling table layout. Below are examples of several different booth layouts to consider for your booth.

The Sampling Layout:

This is the most popular layout for vendors at fairs and festivals. It allows people to view your products and sample your products. As you can see, you are the person behind the table giving the "okay" sign.

The Side Tables:

This is a good table layout to use if you offer a number of products. Unlike the sampling layout, this layout invites customers directly into your tent. If you have a busy show, you may have 2 or 3 people at a given time inside your tent. However, since you have more space to watch, the potential for theft increases with this layout.

The downside of this layout is available "browsing space". If you already have 2 or 3 people inside your tent previewing your products, others may feel uncomfortable entering a tent with so many people and simply continue to walk by. Remember to keep browsing space in mind when using this table layout.

The Flying V:

This is a good table layout to use if you offer a number of products. Like the sampling layout, this layout doesn't invite customers directly into your tent. You can get more people viewing your product with this layout when compared to the side-table layout.

The U-Shape Tables:

Like the side-table layout if you offer a number of products this is a good tent layout. If you have a busy show, you may have 3 or 4 people at a given time inside your tent. However, since you have more space to watch, the potential for theft increases with this layout.

In addition, like the side-table layout if you have a busy show others may feel uncomfortable entering a tent with 3 or 4 other people and simply continue to walk by.

Product photos

Product usage photos are an excellent way to present your products to customers. If appropriate, the best way to use product photos is to hang several 12"x12" or 18"x24" posters along the inside of your tent. Banners are another way to display your products inside your booth. Banners allow you share vital information to your potential customers without taking up limited table space.

We use banners and photos in our booth. We have product usage photos, photos of Hollywood celebrities with our products and more. We have celebrities and professional athletes that have tried and who use our products on a consistent basis.

Having close up of photos, customer testimonials, etc. of your products are also an excellent way to show the features and benefits of your products, too.

"As Seen In"

**Joey Pantoliano
- Sopranos**

**Laura Nelson
- Miss America 2007**

**- Percy
Jackson and
the Lightning
Thief**

"As Seen In"

**Chelsea Hightower
- Dancing with the
Stars**

**Gregory Michael
-Greek**

Below are a few examples how we use our photos in our booth:

Here is what our booth looked like at a recent fair in Northern Michigan. You can see these Hollywood photos on the left hand side of the photo:

Back Banners

In addition to product photos we also have a banner in the back of our tent. Here are a few photos of our tent with and without the back banner.

The first photo is without booth without the back banner, while the second and third photo is with the banner. You can see the difference in the "look and feel" of the booth when we have the banner set up.

Here is the same show with the banner at the back of our booth

Here is another show with everything set up. We have our product photos, our banners and our tent signs. If you walked by our tent you would certainly know exactly what we are offering.

If you notice our banner states "Taste America's #1 Salsa. If you make such a claim make sure you can back it up with proven and credible facts. Here is the background information on our salsas that allow us to make such a claim.

Our salsas were voted #1 in America in National Competition two years in a row in 2007 and 2008! We won first prize at America's Best National Food Competition. This is the largest and more recognized professional food show in the nation. Each year over 1200 companies submit their products into this competition.

In addition, we won 23 national food awards including 18 Scovie Awards.

In addition, here is what Michelle Bommarito, a celebrity chef and frequent guest on the Food Network said about our salsas

"I was so excited to discover your salsa! It's not only great tasting, but full of quality, all-natural ingredients."

Chef Michelle Bommarito, a frequent guest on the Food Network

The Wow Factor

: Mirrors and product samples are what I call the Wow Factor. The Wow Factor allows your customers to experience your product. The Wow Factors helps your customers to see how they will look wearing your hat or sampling your products.

Here are few ideas to incorporate the Wow factor into your booth.

- Mirrors: If you sell products customers can wear like scarves, hats, t-shirts, etc. placing small mirror in your booth. A simple mirror will show help your customers to see how good they will look when they are wearing your product.
- Product sampling: If you sell food products like fudge, popcorn, salsa, etc. you know sampling is an excellent way to sell your product. You know, once people taste your product they will buy it.

Traffic Generation Ideas

Here are few ideas to get people to visit your booth. The purpose of these ideas is to get people to your booth location.

- Place a trash can in front of your booth. Even if you don't offer a food-related product, place a trash can in front of your booth. This is an excellent way to get additional foot traffic. We always have a trash can in front of our booth and we have countless people stopping by to throw trash away and a number of them have also sampled and purchased our product. This will also help to keep the festival grounds clean.

- Be an information booth or offer handouts about the festival. People will visit your booth to learn about the event or grab handouts about the festival. These are simply pamphlets printed by the organizers listing the daily events. Talk with the organizers about offering handouts at your booth.

- Offer free samples. Free samples are a great way to get people into your booth.

- Joint Venture with a local merchant. If you attend the same street fair yearly, you probably meant some of the local merchants of the town. Contact them to place your flyer in their store and in return you pass out one of their flyers to each of your purchases at the festival. We have done this a number of times with the local businesses with good success. Since most of the people attending the festival are local residents, this is a win-win deal.

- Offer a coupon. Offer an instant saving coupon. Let's say your average selling price for your products is $20, you could offer a $5 off coupon when they purchase over $50. This encourages people to buy more from you and you'll soon find people will simply add additional product just to get the $5 discount coupon.

The Festival Profits Lead Generation System

Making a sale at a festival is exciting. No matter how many sales we make at the shows we attend, I still get excited with each and every sale. To me there is something magical about selling my product to a customer. Maybe it's the idea of know that something I have created is going to be enjoyed and appreciated by another human being.

So why not have that same feeling of enjoyment all year long? Thanks to technology, you can be making sales to customers during the off-season and making money year round. It doesn't matter what you sell, customers will buy your products all year long. However, before they can you need to collect their contact information.

In this section you'll ideas you can implement immediately to garner sales from people who bought your product at a show and those who only viewed your products, but didn't buy. In the next several pages, you'll learn a simple step-by-step method in monetize every festival you attend.

The shows we attend range from 5,000 to 70,000 attendees. Of course, we don't expect to sell our products to every person that attends the show, that would be unrealistic but with every show we do increase our year round customer base. You'll learn how to do it too.

You know, selling at a festival is nothing more than a numbers games. Let's say you exhibit at a show that 5,000 attendees you may sell 1% of them your products. This means you would make 50 sales during the event at a selling price of $10 per item. That closing ratio and price may be high or low compared to your product, I don't know but we'll use that number for our example purposes.

In the following pages you'll learn how to increase the number of items you sell throughout the year. Meaning I'm going to give you a proven strategy to increase your sales through the remainder of the year.

Here's an example of how the numbers work:

- 50 pieces sold at the one day show at $10 each: $500 in gross sales

- 50 pieces sold during the remaining year at $10 each: $500 in gross sales for the follow 12 months.

You just doubled your year round income from that same show. Isn't that exciting? Now let's take say you do 10 events a year. How would this strategy impact your bottom line?

50 pieces sold at each show: 500 pieces sold for all ten shows.

$10 per piece sold at each show: $5,000 in gross sales for the 10 shows

After Show Sales:

An additional 500 pieces sold throughout the remaining of the year at $10: An additional $5,000 in gross sales every year. Remember these are additional sales you are making from the comfort of your own home.

Now that you understand how the numbers works, let's learn how to make these additional sales...

Lead Capture Techniques

The following lead capture techniques will allow you to capture contact information from both buyers and non-buyers at the shows you attend and encourage these people to visit your website and buy from you year round.

Create an Email Capture Form - Capture Contact Information Easily

Creating an email list is vital to offering your arts and crafts to your customers year round.

So how do you capture the contact information from attendees visiting your booth? The best way to do this is to offer them a free downloadable report in exchange for their name and email address. The report would be related to your type of business and should contain between15 – 30 pages. The special report would contain tips and additional information related to what you are selling at the street fair.

Simply place a sign-up form on your table with a sign that reads something that is related to what you are selling:

- Sign up to Receive Information about Wood Working Tips
- Sign up to Receive Information about Knitting Secrets
- Sign up to Receive Information about Cooking
- Sign up to Receive Information about Stained Glass

Here is an example of an email capture form:

Sign Up to Receive Free Sewing Tips

Name: Email Address:

When someone writes their name on your email capture form, when you return home you would simply email them the free report. You would place this email capture form in your booth for people to fill out. I've included an example of an email capture form below.

Also, don't worry if you don't like to write or you're unsure how to get started, our company can assist you with implementing all of the strategies in this special module.

For a nominal cost, we can provide you with a personalized downloadable report you can give away to your visitors. To learn more about our report writing services contact us toll-free at 1-877-746-7477. We have writers that can create a report on almost any topic, here are a few examples of topics of downloadable reports we can provide:

- Jewelry
- Recipes books
- Pet related
- Landscaping
- Golf
- Sewing
- Arts and crafts
- And more…

To learn more about this low-cost services, simply call us.

It's that simple. We receive dozens of names and email addresses from both buyers and non-buyers every festival we attend. You simply please this form on your table. Below is an example of where we place our email capture form.

We place our sign form on the left side of our table. This allows us to sample the product on the right-hand side and while the people are waiting for their free sample, they can complete the sign-up form on the left-hand side. We collect dozens of email addresses each show.

Once you collect these names and email address, simply add them into your newsletter service. This will provide you with the contact information in which can send special offers all year round. We use the autoresponder service called Aweber to help us manage our email list.

In the next section, you'll learn more about autoresponder services including Aweber.

Another excellent strategy you can use can provide to the visitors to your booth in exchange for their contact information is to offer an immediate discount in return for their name, address and email address. For example, you could offer them a $1 instant saving coupon when they complete your email capture form. It's that simple.

Offer a Free Downloadable Report to Buyers

In addition to offering a free downloadable report to those who enter their contact information on your email capture form, you also need to offer this same report to those who purchase from you. This is a great way to offer additional value to those people who just gave you money in exchange for your product. The best way to do this is to create bag inserts. A bag insert is simply a printed postcard you give to customer when they purchase from you.

You'll soon find the traffic to your website and your online sales steadily increasing since many may make a purchase directly from your site while they are downloading your free report.

Here is an example of a few of the bag inserts we offer to every person who purchases from us. The first is an example of the free Tart Cherry Health Report, while the second is for a free fruit recipe cookbook.

Two Free Downloadable Books from Traverse Bay Farms / Fruit Advantage

Book #1: Tart Cherry Health
Report -
Learn the natural
health benefits of tart cherries.

Book #2: Fruit Salsa
Recipes -
Over 3 Dozen Fruit
Salsa Recipes

Visit www.TraverseBayFarms.com

Offer a Free Downloadable Report to Non-Buyers

Not every person visiting your booth will purchase your crafts the day of the festival. This may be due to lack of money, lack of time or simply not in the mood to make a purchase. However, they may be interested in purchase something from you a few days after the event.

You would simply offer the free downloadable post card to people who visit your booth but do not buy. Once they visit your website to download the free report, they will be asked to subscribe to your autoresponder email program.

Autoresponders Explained

Obviously, an autoresponder service is the most vital thing. Without it, you won't be able to collect email addresses or email those you collect. There are two types of autoresponder services – hosted and self-hosted.

Self-Hosted

Self-hosted scripts won't typically cost you a monthly fee, but they may cost you an upfront charge for the script itself. However, you may run into some issues that make you wish you'd gone with a hosted service.

First, with hosted scripts, you don't have access to the whitelisted status that many of the hosted services have. This means many of your subscribers won't receive your emails, and instead your messages will go to their spam boxes where they will probably never be seen.

Second, you will be on your own when it comes to dealing with spam complaints. When you are a member of a hosted service, they can handle spam complaints on your behalf. If you use double-opt in so that people have to confirm their request before they are subscribed, you will have extra protection in the case of spam complaints.

However, ISPs may not trust you when you tell them you have a double-opt in from your own script. It may be difficult to prove, and you may run the risk of having your hosting company disconnect your service temporarily, or your domain confiscated by your registrar.

Hosted

Hosted autoresponder services are much safer to use. Not only are they typically whitelisted with most major ISPs, but they will work hard to ensure you are protected in the event that you have any spam complaints.

Popular Hosted Services

There are many different hosted services you could use, but each has their pros and cons. It can be difficult to decide which one to use when you're confronted with dozens of different choices.

I'm going to give you a brief rundown of some of the most popular hosted autoresponder services so you can hopefully choose the right one for your purposes. Remember, if you choose the wrong autoresponder, you will either lose the subscribers you've already collected, or you'll have to transfer them to a new service.

Transferring leads to a new service can be a major hassle. Unless you're already well known with your new service, they may not want to accept your leads at all. And if they do, they may require you to ask all of your leads to reconfirm their subscription.

This could result in leads failing to reconfirm, which could result in a huge reduction in the size of your list. Obviously, that would cost you a lot of hard work building the original list. Thus, it is essential to choose the right service from the start.

Aweber.com – Aweber.com is the most popular autoresponder service among internet marketers. They have pricing plans that will grow with you, so you can pay less when you're just getting started, and you won't have to pay a higher monthly fee until your list grows. They are very easy to use, and are considered extremely reliable.

GetResponse.com – GetResponse.com is very similar to Aweber.com, and they are Aweber's closest competitors among marketers. They also have plans that will grow with your business. They used to be extremely reliable, but many marketers have noticed that their servers are a bit unreliable lately.

iContact.com – iContact.com is not used as commonly by internet marketers, but it is very popular with large corporations such as Coleman, Electrolux, and Frigidaire. Their prices are very competitive, so they are definitely worth considering.

ConstantContact.com – Constant Contact offers similar services to other popular choices, but they also have a free trial. This way, you can try out their service to see if you're happy with it. The main caveat, of course, is that you may feel forced into staying after the trial if you've built a substantial email list, even if you're not quite happy with the service.

MailChimp.com – Mail Chimp is a newer service, and many people are turning to them because they offer a free service. While your list is small, it won't cost you anything. However, there is a laundry list of topics they don't allow, so you have to be very careful to ensure you aren't breaking their terms. It would be very unfortunately to build a decently-sized list and lose it all because you failed to read their rules.

Offer High Value, Free Gifts to Encourage Repeat Business

Repeat business is vital any business. By offering free, high value gifts for repeat business your customers will soon become loyal buyers of your products and services.

In addition to offering a free report to getting people to sign up for your email list, you can also provide free reports to your email list. Your subscribers will be eager to read your email communications if you offer free valuable gifts for them on a regular basis.

The best way to approach your list in providing valuable information and gifts is to understand where they are in the buying process. You need to really think about your customers and what they need to take the next step toward purchasing from your business.

This process is called a sales funnel. For example, let's say you sell wind climes and other outdoor related products.

Here is a series of free and valuable reports you can use to walk them through your sales funnel:

- Report #1: How to Get Your Vacation Home Ready for the Summer
- Report #2: How to Get Birds to Eat from Your Bird Feeders
- Report #3: How to Select the Right Wind Chimes for Your Backyard
- Report #4: How to Winterize Your Vacation Home for the Winter

Each report offers information on specific type of product you offer at your store. All of these reports would have your contact information and a limited time offer to purchase a specific type of product from you.

Spread the Word about your Business and Make it Go Viral

Word of mouth is one of the best ways to get new business. You want your customers to tell their family, friends and co-workers about your business. This is called "going viral".

Here are a few examples you can use to make your business go viral:

- Offer a Refer a Friend service. For example, in my gourmet fruit business we offer a Refer a Friend special worth $18.95. Whenever a current customer refers a friend and that referral makes a purchase over $25, we send the person who gave us the referral a gift worth $18.95.

- Create a how-to video or audio explaining a unique way of doing something. You can simply do this with a video recorder. Once you have created this video, place a link on your website and every email you send out. You learn simple ways to make videos in the video training session of the Festival Profits System. Visit the main download page to learn more about making videos. You received this download page when you made your purchase.

- Give a free coupon worth $5 or $10 to subscribers who get 10 other people to sign up for your email newsletter.

- Include the following message in the signature line your emails and email newsletters: "Feel free to share this valuable information and content with your friends. Simply forward them this email."

Conclusion

I personally wish you the very best in implementing this proven strategies and systems. If you need additional assistance, check out our coaching modules to see how we can help you take your street fair business to the next level. Give us a call to learn more at: 1-877-746-7477

Additional Resources:

Check out these partner sites for additional information in this specific areas:

Start a Food Business – If your friends and family are raving about your recipes, this complete step-by-step course will teach you how to start your own food business for fun and profit in a single weekend. www.StartAFoodBusiness.com

As Seen in Michigan.com – If you have a business in the State of Michigan, you can't afford to miss this… Learn proven strategies to market and grow your business the "Michigan Way" www.MarketingTheMichiganWay.com